Mainstream • Women • Historical • Music CDs

Edit et Cetera Ltd.

Nonfiction • Young Adult • Children • Poetry

presents

PAPILLONS

A Book of Poetry in French & English
by
Clementine de Blanzat

English translations edited by Linda Lane

ISBN: 0-9746122-2-7

Cover Design: Linda Lane
Images from Corel Graphics
© by Clementine de Blanzat & its licensors

Edit et Cetera Ltd., a small publishing company in Grand Junction, Colorado, is pleased to offer a line of books for readers who yearn to enjoy great stories without the explicit sex, gory violence, and bathroom-wall language that permeate so much of today's literature and entertainment. We're calling this line Family Book House. Under its umbrella reside a number of genres — women's fiction, mainstream, love stories (broader category than romance), mystery, suspense, young adult, fantasy, historical fiction, and children's books. Our stories will have family themes and will stress the value of family relationships. Nonfiction and selected volumes of poetry will also be offered.

We hope you are as excited about this new line as we are. Please ask for our Family Book House publications at your local bookstore or look for them at amazon.com.

If you have questions or comments, you may contact this author at clementine@familybookhouse.com. Or visit our website at www.FamilyBookHouse.com.

A poet writes not only for self, but also for others. It has been a great experience to share my poems with many Franco-phones during the past several months. It is my hope that my new readers will find as much pleasure in them as did these faithful ones.

So, sit back, have a cup of your favorite beverage, and enjoy!

Clémentine de Blanzat

My greatest thanks to the Daniel Family for their support.

1) *Un petit livre plein d'émotions et de morceaux de vie.*
   A little book full of emotions and bits of life.
   Danielle D.

2) *Elle parle d'elle, des siens, de nous, de son pays... C'est Magique...*
   She speaks of herself, her family, her country…It's Magic….
   Jean-Marie D.

3) *Ce sont des mots les uns à la suite des autres mais qui avec leurs rimes nous transportent dans la nostalgie, le bonheur et le rêve.*
   These words following one another in rhymes transport us into nostalgia, happiness and dreams.
   Katia D.

4) *Elle nous surprend avec ce recueil de poésie , et arrive a nous toucher quand elle parle des siens. Gageons que la Clémentine devienne un fruit exotique tant les rimes acidulées de celle de Blanzat nous transporte dans ce délicieux voyage.*
   She surprised us with this poetic collection, and is able to touch us. I would bet that this Clémentine will become a sweet exotic fruit, as Blanzat's rhymes transport us into a delicious journey.
   Jean - Yves D.

TABLE OF CONTENTS

Papillons 8
Butterflies 9
Quatre Saisons 10
Four Seasons 11
Requiem pour un Nuage 12
Requien for a Cloud 13
De l'Est à l'Ouest 14
Sunrise, Sunset 15
Le Cygne Digne 16
A Dignified Swan 17
Rue Sans-Soucis 18
No-Worry Street 19
Je me souviens 20
I Remember 21
Le Pêcheur 22
The Fisherman 23
J'ai cherché 24
Searching 25
My Lady 26
My Lady 27
Richesses 28
Riches 29
Sa Patrie 30
His Land 31
Toile d'Araignée 32
Spide Web 33
Le Poseur 34
The Pretender 35
Après l'orage 36
After the Storm 37
La Belle et la Bête 38
Beauty and the Beast 39
A Saute-mouton 40
Leap-frog 41
Le Somnambule 42
The Sleepwalker 43
Ponctuation 44
Pour Tes Yeux 46
For Your Eyes 47
Solitaire 48
Solitaire 49
Papa 50
Papa 51
Maman, J'ai Mal 52
Mama, It Hurts 53
Mélodie en Rose 54
Melody in Pink 55
Le Patriarche 56
The Patriarch 57
Ma joie...c'est Toi 58
My Joy Is You 59
Un Peu, Beaucoup… 60
A Little Bit 61
La Mour et L'Amort 62
Love and Death 63
Aimer c'est Donner 64
To Love Is to Give 65

Quand tu n'es pas là 66
When You're Away… 67
Je veux être 68
I Want to Be… 69
Ce soir 70
Tonight 71
Si… 72
If… 73
Quelque chose 74
Something 75
Toi 76
You 77
L'aller-retour 78
Round trip 79
Quand tu m'écris 80
When You Write 81
Parle Moi 82
Talk to Me 83
Otage 84
Hostage 85
Ouïe, j'écoute 86
I Am Listening… 87
Quel âge avons-nous ? 88
How Old Are We? 89
Jamais…Stop…Toujours…Encore 90
Never…Stop…Always…Again 91
Une vie Irrésistible 92
Irresistible Life 93
Les Vagabondes 94
The Vagabonds 95
Clameur de silence 96
Clamor of Silence 97
Tout comme çà 98
Just Like That 99
Courrier du Cœur 100
Love Mail 101
Reprise 102
I Will Survive 103
Le Blues du Sax 104
Sad Song 105
Douceur du Moment 106
Sweet Moment 107
Myosotis 108
Forget-Me-Not 109
Si j'étais Toi… 110
If I Were You 111
Prend ma main 112
Take My Hand 113
Maladie d'amour 114
Lovesick 115
La femme inachevée 116
Unfinished Woman 117
Mes Amis Intimes 118
My Intimate Friends 119
Créativité 120
Creativity 121

In Memory of Lucienne C. Baré,
whose love, understanding, and faith
in me was an inspiration.

PREFACE

Poetry holds an important place in our lives. It is more than just a literary product; it is the translation of our emotions, our dreams, our pains, and our desires. From its magnified language we arrive at the very source of our actions, thoughts, and feelings.

Everything is poetry material: The Divine, love, pain, human tenderness…or fear, horror, and misery…or the starry sky, rainbows, a pet, a butterfly, a storm, a tear on a child's face, the seasons of our lives.

The saddest thing is to have forgotten. In reality the collective memory of the world is full of poetry.

Poetry is not dead—it only has been sleeping a bit; and it's still a necessity for the human mind, of which it is the most ancient and spontaneous form of expression.

We need poetry so we may laugh and cry, blame and love. It is our messenger and our friend. A book of poetry is nothing less than an open heart, and we need to give it back its place.

In this materialistic and technical world in which we live, we need to read poetry to safeguard our capacity for imagination, dreaming, and enthusiasm…safeguard also our possibilities for escape that we so need from time to time. We find a refuge in the enchanted world of poetry, for there, where all is possible, we can leave behind our daily worries and our anxieties.

Read… Dream… Live…

Clémentine de Blanzat

Papillons

Papillon bleu, Papillon blanc,
D'une fleur à l'autre butinant,
Sur une joue rose pose un baiser;
Dans un calice va s'reposer.

Papillon soleil, Papillon miel,
En cercles d'or danse pour sa belle.
Dans sa robe aux boutons-d'or
Tout ébloui, ses yeux l'adorent.

Papillon nuit, Papillon gris,
Doux comme la mousse il nous sourit
Sous les rayons d'une lune d'argent,
Dans les étoiles du firmament.

Papillon Soie, dans mes pensées,
Comme un printemps plein de muguet.
Rempli mon cœur d'une chanson,
Que seuls connaissent mes Papillons.

C. D. B.

Butterflies

Blue Butterfly, White Butterfly,
Go feasting from daisy to rose,
On a flower's cheek deposit a kiss
And in its chalice take sweet repose.

Sunny Butterfly, Honey Butterfly,
In a golden circle dance
For her in her buttercup dress,
Your eyes dazed with romance.

Night Butterfly in a gray moth's suit
Soft as moss, he rides the wind high,
Smiling to the silver moon's rays
And to the white stars in the sky.

Silky Butterfly from my inner thoughts,
Like a spring bloom under bright skies,
Filling my heart with a sweet song
Known only by my Butterflies.

C.D.B.

Quatre Saisons

Tu es le Printemps de mes jours d'Avril,
Tu remplies mes nuits de sourires fleuris.
Timides violettes, soleils de jonquilles,
Nous fournissent douceur et parfum d'un lit.

Tu es mon Eté aux heures de soleil,
Au bord d'un lac bleu, je peux te bercer.
Les oiseaux du ciel, le buzz d'une abeille,
De leurs chansons d'ailes vont nous emporter.

Tu es mon Automne aux couleurs vibrantes,
Mes bras recevant ta palette d'amour;
D'hier à demain tu me rends vivante
Et mon cœur divague de tes aller r'tours.

Tu es mon Hiver sur un tapis blanc,
Un feu pétillant, tu veux faire câlin;
L'odeur des châtaignes ajoute au roman,
Une année si belle, un amour sans fin.

C. D. B.

Four Seasons

You're the Spring of my April days,
Your smile's blossom the dark night fills,
A scented bed of softness we're offered
By shy violets and sweet daffodils

You're my Summer and I embrace you
On the shore of the lake in the sun;
Heaven's birds and the buzzing bees
Support us on their wings of song.

You're my Autumn, rich with warm color,
Your passion's palette I dream of,
You fill all my days with life,
I'm drunk with the wine of your love.

You're my Winter on a white carpet,
We cuddle and watch the fire dance,
Fragrant chestnuts roast as we ponder
Another year of endless romance.

C. D. B

Requiem pour un Nuage

Etant né d'une mer tranquille,
Eclatante était ta douceur.
Sur cette terre ton ombre subtile
Gentiment effaçait la chaleur.

Tout en riant tu m'amusais,
Changeant tes formes au court du vent,
Même quelques fois je devinais
Qui tu étais pour un instant.

Puis d'un moment devenu triste,
D'un voile de deuil tu t'es couvert.
Le ciel grondait à prendre un risque,
C'est à ta mort que tu pleurais.

As-tu senti mes larmes, Chéri?
D'amour sincère elles sont versées;
Sur ton visage mouillé de pluie,
Ce qu'il me reste d'un cœur blessé.

C. D. B.

Requiem for a Cloud

Born out of a tranquil sea,
You brought softness to the land,
Where your subtle shadow
Gently shaded the sand.

In fun you played with me,
Shape-shifting with whimsies of wind;
Sometimes I could even guess
What you were and what you had been.

Without warning you grew gloomy,
Behind sadness sought to hide,
The sky roared thund'rously
While to your death you cried.

Can you feel my tears, my dear,
On your face wet from the rain?
For a lost love they pour out
From a heart weighed down with pain.

C.D.B.

De l'Est à l'Ouest

L'un connaît le Soleil Levant
L'autre connaît le Soleil Couchant,
Deux points diamétralement opposés
Jamais ne pourront se rencontrer.

Dans cet abîme qui les sépare
Existe même une chose bien rare,
Sans un espoir de se trouver
Ils continuent à se chercher.

Ils se connaissent depuis toujours,
Donne le soleil au petit jour;
Quand la journée est achevée
L'autre doucement va se coucher.

Des mots de couleur ils échangent
Qui pour un peintre sont un challenge.
C'est évident qu'ils ne peuvent pas
L'un sans l'autre faire un pas.

Sommes-nous comme ça, oui, toi et moi?
Dans le soleil j'entends ta voix,
Au crépuscule quand je m'éteins
A toi je pense…te donne demain.

C.D.B.

Sunrise, Sunset

One knows the Sunrise,
The other, the Sunset,
Diametrically opposed,
They never have met.

In this chasm between them,
In unusual harmony,
Each longs to touch the other,
But each knows it cannot be.

Eternally tied together,
One rises to light the dawn,
And when the day is over,
The other one lies down.

They speak in colorful words
The artist cannot portray,
When one of them makes a move
The other's pulled along the way.

Are we like this, you and I?
In the Sunrise you come in view,
Then at twilight when I fade out,
I think of tomorrow…and you.

C.D.B.

Le Cygne Digne

Comme un nuage couvert
De léger duvet blanc,
Il glisse sur l'eau claire
Comme poussé par le vent.

Il vous donne l'impression
Du calme personnifié,
Vous gardez cette vision
Un tableau de beauté.

Mais si vous persévérez
Et regardez plus près,
Sous les plumes lissées
Deux pattes gigotaient.

Ce calme si apparent
Etait là pour tromper.
Il cache bien souvent
L'angoisse qui peut blesser.

Nous sommes bien ainsi,
Aux pensées tourmentées.
Mais pour l'amour d'autrui,
Nous portons ce duvet.

C.D.B.

A Dignified Swan

Covered by a cloud
Of soft white down,
He glides on the water
As though blown around.

At first glance he seems
To be tranquility,
A vision of quietude,
A work of art is he.

But take a look beneath
The calm he'd have you see,
Feet that paddle madly
Belie serenity.

The unruffled façade
Hides dark reality
Of a heart's that wounded
From those who would not see

We are like this, you and I,
In the torment of our minds,
But out of love for others
Our down coats we hide behind.

C.D.B.

Rue Sans-Soucis

Voulez-vous connaître un chemin parfumé ?
Couvert de fleurs et de regards aimés,
Aucun bruit, de machines ou de guerre,
Seul un lézard fuyant dans les bruyères.

Qui ne voudrait pas fuir ce monde lamentable
Et s'asseoir, souriant, ses pieds sous la table;
Devant un vrai banquet de ses mets préférés
Avec tous ses amis, sans jamais se presser.

Au réveil du matin, le corps plein d'énergie
Nous pourrions cultiver un jardin plein de vie,
Et toujours partager les fruits de nos labeurs
Avec milliers, de nos chers frères et sœurs.

Le fait que nous serons d'esprit et de corps sains,
Jamais plus, les douleurs ne nous prendront la main.
Mais le cœur plein de joie nous vivrons tous ensemble
Sans penser que Tel soit, d'une couleur différente.

Voici l'itinéraire de la Rue Sans-Soucis :
Avec une connaissance de Vérité acquise,
Tout d'abord sur la droite vous devez vous tourner
Et puis continuez tout droit, le passé oubliez.

C.D.B.

No-Worry Street

Would you delight in thoughts of dear friends
As you walk down a flowered garden path?
With no sounds of machines or of war,
Just a lizard as it runs through the grass?

Would you leave this old world behind you
For a table filled with favorite delights?
You could share it with those who love you
And it would satisfy all appetites.

Do you want to wake refreshed in the morning
And plant a garden that's brimming with life?
Would you contentedly share its bounty
With brother and sister, husband or wife?

Do you want strength of body and mind?
Would you like pain to be lost in the past?
And all races to live as one family
In a place of joy unsurpassed?

Let me take you to No-Worry Street
Where Knowledge and Truth intertwine,
Turn Right and go straight ahead,
And leave whatever you were behind.

C.D.B.

Je me souviens

Te souviens-tu de nos beaux jours?
Combien de fois, combien de tours
Nos cœurs heureux ont fait l'amour?

Te souviens-tu un jour d'été?
Dans tes bras forts tu m'as portée
Un monde nouveau nous avions fait.

Te souviens-tu de nos baisers,
De notre amour qui nous berçait,
La douce chaleur qui nous couvrait?

Toutes nos promesses, as-tu oublié?
Un nœud au cœur tu m'as donné;
Retourne à celle qui veut t'aimer….
Je me souviens.

C.D.B

I Remember

Do you remember those days?
How many times, how many ways
Our happy hearts would fall in love?

Do you remember a summer day?
In your strong arms you took me away
To the brand new world all our own.

Do you remember the love that cradled us?
The warm softness that covered us?
Do you remember our kisses?

Have you forgotten the words you said?
Or are you breaking my heart instead?
Return to me, my love.
I remember…

C.D.B

Le Pêcheur

Sous le soleil marin où tu jetais ta ligne,
Ta belle peau basanée buvait ses rayons d'or.
Au bout de l'horizon qui veut garder sa ligne
Ta vie aimait flotter de ce point jusqu' alors.

Le long des Côtes d'Espagne et jusqu'à l'Italie,
La Méditerranée t'a porté et bercé,
Pour toi les Côtes de France étaient les plus jolies,
Elles t'ont tendu les bras et tu y es resté.

Sur ses plages douces et blondes, au sein de son Eté,
Tu continues à boire l'azur de son ciel clair.
La houle de la Mer te donne un goût salé
Comme un baiser d'amour qui ne voulait se taire.

C.D.B

The Fisherman

Under the sea's sun where you cast your line
Your bronzed skin drank the golden rays;
But beyond the far horizon
You soared to a shore far away.

Taking you to Spain and Italy,
The Mediterranean showed you their charms,
But the coast of France you found most lovely,
Reaching out with its open arms.

As the sun bathed its blonde beaches
You drank of its azure sky,
The swelling sea gave you salty kisses
Of a love that never would die.

C.D.B

J'ai cherché

J'ai dû chercher l'amour, voulant te le donner,
Milliers d'étoiles, me suis vue traverser.
La belle Amazone ne pouvait me l'offrir,
Arrivée à Florence, la nuit venait mourir.

Les amants de Paris ne pouvaient m'informer,
Les jardins de Versailles m'ont seulement fait rêver.
J'ai donc pensé, qu'il n'était pas pour moi
Et que la vie, m'en donn'rait pas le droit.

Un nouveau jour est là, et soudain,
Une vision douce, un murmure du matin,
D'un œil aveugle a déchiré le voile,
M'a révélé l'espoir trouvé dans les étoiles.

Un torrent jaillissant, très vite m'a inondée,
Le souffle me manquait, je croyais me noyer.
De tes yeux me venait un regard émouvant
Cet amour impossible, que je cherchais longtemps.

La pointe de ma plume, d'un geste délicat
A ramassé de suite le bonheur de ma voix,
Et d'une main de velours l'a posé sur ton cœur;
L'amour que je cherchais, vient de toi, ma douceur.

C.D.B

Searching

Searching for a Love to share,
I crossed thousands of stars above,
The great Amazon could not help me,
Even in Florence, I found no love.

Paris lovers could not make it happen,
Versailles' Gardens were not for me,
I resigned my heart to loneliness
And a life where love would not be.

Then a new day came from tomorrow,
A soft vision, a whisper at dawn
Took hopelessness out of my sorrow
And brought the joy of love in the morn.

A torrent flooded my being,
I gasped and thought I would drown,
Your eyes told me you had been waiting,
Right here my Love I had found.

I sat down to write of my pleasure,
The happiness flowed from my pen,
Now tuck it away in your heart,
For I found you, my Love, my friend.

C.D.B

My Lady

Quand je te vois si belle
La tête dans les nuages;
Ton regard gris surveille
De la Seine son passage.

Je t'ai toujours aimée
Depuis ma tendre enfance.
Plus d'une fois j'ai pensé
A ton acierique élégance.

Depuis bien des années
Tu es restée fidèle
A ton Paris charmé
Par ta pose citadelle.

Ils viennent du monde entier
De l'Est à l'Ouest, du Sud au Nord.
Pour te toucher et t'admirer,
Mais t'oublier ?...Que dans la mort!

C. D. B.

My Lady

When I look at your elegant beauty,
Your head reaching into the sky,
I see your grey eyes watching
The Seine River flowing by.

I have always loved you
From my most tender years,
Thinking often of your lacework
And the strength of your steel tiers.

Your years have now been many,
You've faithfully watched below,
A sentinel over Paris,
As generations come and go.

They come from the world over,
From North, South, East, and West,
To caress you and admire you,
And they'll remember...until death.

C.D.B.

Richesses

Combien pour la nuit vêtue d'étoiles?
Ce firmament qui m'émerveille,
Combien pour la mer qui roule son voile
De bleu, d'argent et de soleil?

Combien pour l'oiseau qui chante au matin?
Que même Mozart ne peut copier,
Combien pour le petit chaton malin
Qui court et joue dans mes papiers?

Chaque jour nous devenons un miracle
Dans notre corps qui est si beau.
Pensons même à ce spectacle
Que nous trouvons dans le cerveau.

Le temps lui-même est un mystère,
Mais nous l'avons à notre portée.
Demandons-nous qui est ce Père
Si généreux, et plein de bonté?

De beauté, nous sommes entourés,
La vie nous berce, nous change, nous donne,
Tout est gratuit, nous sommes comblés
De ces Richesses, et l'Amour qui nous étonne.

Oui, chacun est Riche, sans un effort.
Tendre la main est le seul geste,
Puis nous prenons, toujours et encore.
Mon Dieu, Merci, pour ta Sagesse!!

C.D.B.

Riches

What is the cost of a starry night
From the depths of endless time?
How much for the sea whose waves enfold
Shades of silver and blue and sunshine?

How much for the song of the bird at dawn
To whom Mozart could not reply?
How much for the kitten playing on my desk
Who turns my pen and papers awry?

Each day we become a miracle,
Our bodies such wisdom contain,
Our minds and thoughts just a bit
Of the power that resides in our brain.

The mystery of passing time
Governs our days and years.
Who is it that gives us this gift,
A lifetime for joys and tears?

By beauty we are surrounded,
Life moves us in many ways,
We are showered by love and riches
From One kindly filling our days.

Oh, yes, we are rich without effort,
We need only reach out to receive;
We thank you, dear God, for your Wisdom
That you offer to each one for free!

C.D.B.

Sa Patrie

Des Montagnes et des Vallées
De grands Lacs et des Rivières,
Le Grand Esprit lui a donné
Un beau pays dont il est fier.

Au cours des temps il a connu
Tous les bienfaits d'une vie bénie,
Souvent chassant à demi nu
Le Bison brun dans les prairies.

D'une terre fertile il se soignait,
Sa méd'cine pratique j'ai appris,
Savoir et sagesse je connais,
Et de cela, le remercie.

Un autre vola sa liberté
En occupant " La Terre Promise "
Du brave Indien ne s'est soucié,
Vallées, Montagnes ont été prises.

C.D.B.

His Land

Mountains and their lush valleys
Running rivers and silver blue lakes...
The Great Spirit had kindly given him
   The pride of his own Estate.

As time passed, he grew in knowledge,
   Learned secrets of a blessed life,
   Half naked he hunted the bison,
With his bow and arrow and knife.

From the earth he healed himself,
   His medicine I have learned,
His knowledge and wisdom I found,
And for that, my respect he earned.

But another stole his freedom
And occupied his "Promised Land,"
His mountains and valleys were taken
And he became a homeless man.

C.D.B.

31

Toile d'Araignée

Cette toile si fine et si légère
De dentelle et perles d'argent,
Sous la rosée de l'aube claire
S'agrippe au cœur de son amant.

C'est avec soin qu'elle est tissée,
De doigts agiles devient merveille.
Les yeux du cœur elle fait tourner,
Et tout d'un coup rien n'est pareil.

Une coquine pleine de surprises
Sait se servir de sa beauté.
Il le veut bien, et sans reprise,
Il la laisse prendre sa liberté.

Enveloppé de cette mousseline
Perdant de vue sa raison d'être,
Une caresse, le cœur trépigne,
En elle il meurt, pour se renaître.

C.D.B.

Spider Web

She weaves her web so fine
Of silver pearls and lace,
In the dew of early morn
Her lover's heart embraced.

With great care she is weaving,
Nimble fingers magic make,
His heart she turns toward her
Suddenly, she's on the take.

She is naughty and coquettish,
With her beauty she holds sway,
He is willing to do her bidding,
And his freedom she takes away.

Entangled in the muslin web,
He will forget his life alone,
Her caress has his heart jumping,
In her he dies and they are one.

C.D.B.

Le Poseur

Avec la tête penchée,
Un Saule pleureur se tient
Tel un enfant gâté,
Il pleure plutôt pour rien.

Quelles raisons a-t-il donc
Pour se sentir si triste?
Il a tout, un beau tronc,
Une rivière qui court vite.

Il sait bien qu'il est beau,
Son nom n'est pas Pleureur;
Il s'admirait dans l'eau,
C'est simplement Orgueil!

C.D..B.

The Pretender

With his head bent over
A Weeping Willow stands,
Just as a spoiled child does,
His sadness he pretends.

Just what reason does he have
To cry out and to complain?
He has it all, the grandest trunk,
At his roots, a running stream.

He knows well his beauty,
Weeping is not his fame.
At himself he still is gazing,
Prideful, justly, is his name.

C.D.B.

Après l'orage

Les nuages lourds poussent un soupir;
L'air est épais et grince des dents.
Ses yeux farouches comme un délire
Lancent des éclairs, deviennent mordants.

Depuis des jours il mijotait,
Le vent mouillé crachait des larmes.
Quel sale tonnerre va éclater;
Je prends couvert ; sauver mon âme.

En restant calme je le regarde,
Deux grands yeux noirs me déchiraient.
Il n'est pas beau quand il s'emballe
Mais devant lui….Je souriais.

Après son tonnerre, ses éclairs d'acier,
La pluie de mon cœur adoucit sa voix;
Laisse mon arc-en-ciel, son front caresser
Et l'apprivoiser comme la dernière fois.

C.D.B.

After the Storm

Heavy clouds let out a sigh,
Thick air grinds noisy teeth,
Out of angry thunderheads
Lightning strikes the world beneath.

After simmering for days,
A wet wind pours out its tears,
Thunder growls its vengeance
And for my life I fear.

But in calmness I confront him
Black eyes glare back at me;
He's ugly when he's raging,
Yet I smile for him to see.

After his bellows and cutting flashes,
Rain from my heart softens his roar;
His forehead the rainbow caresses
And he's tamed once more as before.

C.D.B.

La Belle et la Bête

Une petite frisée, une crème de Bijou,
Ses yeux, doucement, elle fixe sur toi;
Elle a fait sa niche, là, sur tes genoux
Sentant comme une peur, tristesse qui te boit.

Tout comme moi aussi, elle veut te parler
Mais tu restes sourd à celle qui t'aime.
Ses yeux pleins de larmes elle ne peut fermer,
Et sa petite patte sur ta main elle mène.

Un petit mot doux, un joli sourire
Lui ferait plaisir, la rendrait vivante;
Elle veut t'emmener au jardin courir
Mais tu fais la moue, et elle reste aimante.

C.D.B.

Beauty and the Beast

My crème de la crème, my sweet poodle,
Watches you with the kindest expression,
On your lap she tries to bring comfort
And release you from your depression.

Just as I do, she wants to reach out,
But you, Love, won't hear us today,
Her eyes overflow with her sadness
When you push her small paw away.

A kind word or even a smile
Would do much to brighten her day,
She wants to romp, but you're pouting,
And she loves you, so with you she'll stay.

C.D.B.

A Saute-mouton

Les cris, les rires d'années passées,
Quand les petits venaient jouer
Des jeux d'été, des jeux d'enfants,
Ils dépensaient si bien leur temps.
Les cris, les rires d'années passées…

Les regardant, je me souviens
De souvenirs des jours anciens.
De tous ces jours mon préféré,
Le Saute-mouton, j'ai bien aimé.
Les regardant je me souviens….

Dans les prairies vertes et fleuries,
Nos pensées claires et sans soucis,
Les jeunes gazelles que nous étions
Pendant des heures : Petits moutons
Dans les prairies vertes et fleuries….

Quel d'entre nous n'a pas d'obstacle?
Ne pouvant pas faire de miracles,
Jour après jour nous les voyons,
Les évitons à Saute-mouton.
Quel d'entre nous n'a pas d'obstacle?...

Bien des ennuis et préjudices
Nous pourrions prendre bien au sérieux;
Mais joie de vivre ne pourrions suivre,
A Saute-mouton, nous vivons mieux;
Sans autre ennuis ou préjudices….

C.D.B.

Leap-frog

From years past, the screams and laughs
When little ones would come to play
Summer games and Winter crafts...
I recall exuberant days
From years past, the screams and laughs...

Watching them, I am reminded
Of the games I used to play,
Of all these my very favorite
Was leap-frog, I have to say
Watching them I am reminded...

In the meadows green and blooming,
We'd run carefree and pretend,
Like gazelles we leapt and played
Little Froggies for hours on end
In the meadows green and blooming...

Obstacles forever face us,
But miracles we cannot do,
When solutions don't come to us,
We leap-frog like we used to,
Obstacles cannot destroy us...

Many worries, woes, and hurdles
Would take the joy from every day,
We can avoid this troubling fate
When leap-frog we choose to play,
Without worries, woes, or hurdles...

C.D.B.

Le Somnambule

Il marchait dans la vie
D'un pas incertain,
Connaissant de la nuit
Que son triste refrain.

Les pensées chiffonnées
Par des voiles d'ignorance,
Essayant de raisonner
Sur un monde d'espérance.

Dans son sommeil épais
Il ne pouvait comprendre.
Ses notions l'enterraient,
Ne pouvant s'faire comprendre.

Lumière du Dieu Céleste
Ouvre bien grand ses yeux;
De ton amour, d'un geste
Tu peux le rendre heureux.

Sur tes chants de sagesse
Il s'est vu retourner.
Courant à toute vitesse,
Pour ne plus s'égarer.

C.D.B.

The Sleepwalker

He walks through his life
With an uncertain gait,
Knowing the sadness
The night can relate.

His thoughts are confused
By his ignorance,
His reasoning flawed
By permissiveness.

Walking in his sleep,
He does not comprehend,
Buried beneath his thoughts,
He never takes a stand.

Oh, Light of Celestial Love,
Please open his eyes to see,
From the depths of your affection
Please wake him and set him free.

He hears your songs of wisdom,
He learns your righteous ways,
You woke him from his slumber,
He will serve you all his days.

C.D.B.

Ponctuation

Voici une triste histoire
Entre les Parenthèses,
Elles ne faisaient que boire
Les mots de leur ivresse.

Chez l'accent Circonflexe
Elles ont traîné les pieds.
L'une et l'autre se vexent
Même se mettent à crier.

La Virgule et le Point
Appellent le Trait d'Union
Qui ne suivait pas loin
Sifflotant sa chanson.

Mademoiselle Cédille
Dans toute sa sagesse
Observant ces débiles,
Décide que cela cesse.

Vous ! Qui êtes dans la cave!
Vous avez assez bu,
Soyez donc l'Accent Grave,
Et vous, à droite, l'Accent Aigu.

C. D. B.

44

Punctuation
Due to the different punctuation marks used in the French
language, this poem does not lend itself
to an English rendition.

Pour Tes Yeux

Si beau et calme tu l'étais,
Quand tes beaux yeux me regardaient,
Mon regard ne les quittait pas,
Amour profond j'avais pour toi.

Le plaisir de t'avoir à moi,
Te garder blotti dans mes bras;
Mots d'amour tu ne pouvais dire
Mais tes yeux étaient tout sourire.

Ta petite main serrant un doigt
De ma main qui n'te quittait pas,
Un petit homme aux yeux d'émail
Pour un moment, petite canaille.

Les années passent, tu as grandit
Sans même savoir tu as compris
Que tes beaux yeux les femmes adorent,
Et que maman n'avait pas tort.

Même aujourd'hui je les revois
Tes yeux d'amandes comme autrefois,
Ils m'ont fait rire, m'on fait pleurer
Et même aussi, mon cœur brisé.

Et j'aime toujours te regarder,
Sans dire un mot tu peux parler
Avec tes yeux et ton sourire,
Et je n'veux pas te voir partir.

C. D. B.

For Your Eyes

So calm and handsome you were
When your eyes would stare at me,
And I would return your gaze,
My sweet love with eyes of green.

I knew that you were mine...
If only for a while,
You knew no words to speak
But your eyes were full of smile.

Your small hand around the finger
Of my hand holding on to you,
A little man with enamel eyes
Who's sometimes a bit naughty, too.

Years have passed, you've grown up,
And now you are able to tell...
Women love your beautiful eyes,
And your Mama knew it so well.

Even today when I see them,
Almond eyes make me laugh and cry,
Sometimes my heart is broken,
Sometimes it is flying high.

I still love looking at you,
Without words you speak to me
With your smile and with those eyes...
I wish you would never leave.

C.D.B.

Solitaire

Une rencontre plutôt banale
Sur la mousse d'un tapis vert,
Cinquante quatre autour d'une table
Prêts à jouer Solitaire.

Le cœur coupant que tu montrais
M'effrayait peu, comme tu as vu;
Puis nos regards se sont croisés,
Ta Dame de Cœur suis devenue.

Les heures, les jours ont vite passés
Creusant au Pic des souvenirs.
Souvent Joker tu d'vais trouver,
Le dernier mot tu voulais dire.

Avec un Bang ! Tu m'as surprise,
Une bague au doigt avec tes vœux;
Dame de Diamant, petite marquise,
Tout éblouis étaient mes yeux.

Et tout heureux nous sommes partis
Pour la Valet des Trèfles doux.
Dans cette première de paradis
Cet amour vrai nous rendait fous.

Et pour couronner notre histoire;
Même si elle vous a amusés,
Je suis bénie, non pas une fois
Mais quatre petits As, il m'a donné.

C.D.B.

Solitaire

On a mossy green carpet
With quite a casual air,
Fifty four around a table
Wait to play Solitaire.

The cutting heart you were showing
Didn't scare me, as you could see;
But then our looks kept on crossing...
Your Queen of Hearts I came to be.

After that the time passed quickly
With Spade planting memories;
And Joker you would pull out,
The last word was yours to be.

Then out of the blue you surprised me,
With a ring on my finger, your vow,
Queen of Diamonds, little marquise,
I was totally bedazzled now!

We went on to be truly happy,
King and Queen of Hearts were we,
Even though our love made us crazy,
A paradise it proved to be.

The crowning joy of our loving story —
Did you find it amusing in places? —
I have been blessed several times over,
For you've given me four little Aces.

C.D.B.

Papa

Si seulement j'avais pu te garder
Plus près de moi toutes ces années.
Mais la vaste mer nous séparait,
Si seulement nous étions hier.

Tu es parti trop tôt pour moi
Sans pouvoir être avec toi.
C'est difficile de me convaincre
Je n'connaitrais plus ton étreinte.

Mais maintenant tu n'souffres plus
Dans le silence de l'inconnu.
Un jour viendra où finalement
Je pourrai t'aimer comme avant.

Le souffle de vie te reviendra
De tes yeux bleus tu me verras,
Nous pourrons rire comme jadis
Sur la terre neuve d'un paradis.

Papa, tu me manques.

C.D.B.

Papa

If only you could have been closer
As the last years slipped away,
But the great sea lay between us,
And we had only yesterdays.

You left long before I was ready
To say my good-byes to you,
Now it's so hard to believe
Your loving hugs have gone away, too.

Even though you no longer suffer
In the silence of the unknown,
The day will come when you'll learn
That the pain of death's overthrown.

Life will once more be yours,
Your blue eyes will see me again,
Together we'll laugh as we used to
And share the joys of paradise then.

Papa, I miss you.

C.D.B.

Maman, J'ai Mal

Je t'en pris, dis moi que faire?
S'il te plaît aides moi, ma Mère.
Tu dois connaître un moyen de guérir
Ce mal qui me mange et qui ne veut partir.

Tu m'as dit bien des fois ces jours arriv'raient.
Ne leur fais pas confiance : Sans cesse tu me disais;
Tous ces mots, de promesses et de vœux
N'écoute pas, car il y aura toujours mieux.

Mais maman, dis-moi, est-ce qu'il t'est arrivé?
Ton cœur un jour, soudain'ment te quitter
Pour rencontrer un autre au sourire désarmant
Et ta vie devenue une fable d'enfant.

Un jour tu te sens vide, ne peux vivre sans lui,
Le lendemain tu flottes au ciel du paradis.
Un soir d'amour tu sais que tout cela est vrai;
Mais la rosée de l'aube vient pour tout effacer.

Comme arracher le cœur du fond de mes entrailles
Un amour comme cela ne peut que faire du mal.
Maman, si tu étais auprès de moi, ce soir
Seul un bisou de toi, fini mon désespoir.

C.D.B.

Mama, It Hurts

What can I do? I beg you, tell me,
Some way to heal you must know,
Please, dear Mother, help me,
This pain won't let me go.

You told me such days would come,
Don't trust them, you would say,
Vows are just words, so don't listen,
For better will come your way.

Mother, did it happen to you sometime?
Did your heart on its own take a chance?
Did it fall for a charming smile
And expect a fairy tale romance?

Did you think you can't live without him
And float on soft clouds in the air?
Did you know loving nights that were real
And awake to find nothing there?

I feel like my heart's been torn from me,
This kind of love can bring only pain,
Mom, if tonight you were with me,
With a kiss you could heal me again.

C.D.B.

Mélodie en Rose

Petits chaussons roses sur des pieds de Bébé,
Une jolie bouche en cœur, un petit bouton d'nez.
Son sourire adorable qui veut vous faire pleurer
De joie indestructible qu'elle saura vous donner.

La Rose de toutes les roses que l'on ne doit cueillir,
Mais prendre sa petite main à jamais la chérir.
La plus belle des fleurs qui bientôt se déchire,
Non seulement s'est fanée mais bientôt va mourir.

Donnez-moi une rose d'une journée de printemps
La mettre dans un vase, la protéger du vent,
Elle se penche doucement sur un visage d'enfant
Qui n'a jamais connu l'amour de sa Maman…

C. D. B.

Melody in Pink

Small pink booties on Baby's feet,
Heart shaped mouth and button nose,
Her sweet smile brings tears of joy
That spring forth for the baby Rose.

I touch this flower I cannot pick,
Take her hand and hold in my heart
The fragile blossom fading away
And know that soon we must part.

Ah, the sweet Rose of April,
Safe from whimsies of Spring,
Looks down from the vase on the child
Who never knew the love Mama would bring.

C.D.B.

Le Patriarche

Grand-papa, grand, impressionnant,
Un regard d'acier, sourire désarmant.
Il plaisait aux femmes de la grande ville,
Mais il aimait les petites filles.

Pourquoi étais-je ta préférée?
Plus que les autres, tu m'as gâtée.
Disant : tu vaux ton poids en Or.
Mais je voulais te voir dehors.

Pourtant je t'ai aimé innocemment
Sans comprendre tout ce tourment.
Tu m'as volé ma joie d'enfance,
Tout en violant mon innocence.

J'étais ton jouet de plaisir
Le plus sinistre, je peux dire.
Comment ai-je vécue si longtemps
Avec ce secret si troublant?

De l'automne de ma vie, je vois
Mon printemps fané, mais des fois
Les souffrances de ces années,
Me rendent forte…inébranlable.

C.D.B.

The Patriarch

Grandpa was tall and impressive,
A look of steel with a disarming smile;
He was loved by uptown ladies,
But he liked the very young gals.

Why did you choose me as favorite?
More than others, you chose to spoil me.
To you, I must have been treasure,
But from you I longed to be free.

I loved you as one does her grandpa,
Not grasping this dreadful distress,
My childhood innocence you'd stolen
With the sting of your ugly caress.

I was a pawn for your pleasure,
But your sinister secret I kept,
All my life I have lived with its pain
While the child within me has wept.

In the autumn of my life I can see
My springtime was ripped by your sin,
But all these long years I have suffered
Made me stronger, and this fight I'll win.

C.D.B.

Ma joie...c'est Toi

Mon cœur fond dans des pensées de Toi
Et je me glisse dans des frissons d'amour;
Tant que ma vie sera de Toi et Moi
Jours après nuits le ciel sera toujours.

Tu sais me dire ces mots qui font rêver,
Je m'abandonne à la valse de ta voix;
Dans une danse que je n'peux arrêter
Je peux t'aimer de plus en plus chaque fois.

D'un baiser doux tu me fermes les yeux,
Dans un brouillard d'émotions et de joie,
Je veux toucher ta bouche au délice mielleux,
Et boire ton âme pour couvrir mon émoi.

Comment as-tu fait çà ? Me rendre si fragile.
Dans tes mains je ne suis qu'une poupée,
Dans ta douceur bleutée tu deviens impossible
Et dans tes yeux d'amour, me ravie de jouer.

Page après page je veux parler de Toi,
De l'artiste subtil qui m'a donné la vie;
Les heures n'existent plus dans le creux de tes bras
Et je souhaite ne jamais écrire le mot " Fini."

C.D.B.

My Joy Is You

My heart melts when I think of you
And I tingle with shivers of love,
As long as you're part of my life,
Night's warm skies are always above.

My heart waltzes when I hear your voice,
Your words, my dreams are made of,
Our dance of passion goes on and on,
And my heart keeps falling in love.

With a kiss you are closing my eyes,
I'm in a trance of joy and devotion,
Tasting the honey dew from you lips,
Drinking your soul to soothe my emotion.

You make me so weak and submissive,
I am but a rag doll in your arms,
In your sweetness you become my zenith,
Your eyes twinkle and I fall for your charms.

Page after page, I write of your virtue,
The subtle artist who's painting my life,
In your warm embrace my days are renewed,
May I never write "The End" as your wife.

C.D.B.

Un Peu, Beaucoup...

Je n'étais qu'un petit "Peu"
Seule, une ombre dans tes yeux.
Pensante, un peu timide,
Je flottais comme dans un vide.

Maintenant, je suis "Beaucoup"
Je t'envois un baiser doux,
Et de mon cœur te remercie
Pour cet amour si plein de vie.

Peut-être un jour "Passionnément"
Nous sourirons en nous aimant,
Et voir combien ce petit "Peu "
Bien tendrement devint "Nous Deux."

C.D.B.

A Little Bit

I used to be just a "Little Bit,"
Only a shadow in your eyes,
Pensive and a bit timid,
So lost in empty skies.

Now I have become "Much,"
And I send you a gentle kiss,
Deep in my heart I thank you
For a love and a life of bliss.

Maybe someday in our passion
We will smile as often we do,
To see how "Much" this "Little Bit"
Has tenderly become "we two."

C.D.B.

La Mour et L'Amort

L'amour est foudroyant
La mort aussi.
L'amour nous coupe le souffle
La mort aussi.
L'amour nous vole le cœur
La mort aussi.
L'amour nous anéantit
La mort aussi.
L'amour nous emprisonne
La mort aussi.
L'amour prend notre dernière larme
La mort aussi.
L'amour nous donne sérénité
La mort aussi
L'amour nous dévêtit
La mort aussi.
L'amour nous fait renaître
La mort aussi.
Laisse-moi mourir d'Amour avec toi.

C.D.B.

Love and Death

Love knocks us over,
So does death;
Love takes our breath away,
So does death;
Love steals our heart,
So does death;
Love wrecks us,
So does death;
Love imprisons us,
So does death;
Love takes our last tear,
So does death;
Love gives us serenity,
So does death;
Love strips us bare,
So does death;
Love gives us a new life,
So can death;
Let me love you to death tonight.

C.D.B.

Aimer c'est Donner

Je veux te donner une montagne
Où tu pourrais bien te cacher.
Petit endroit tranquille et calme,
Pour tes besoins d'sérénité.

Aussi décrocher l'Arc-en-ciel,
Le mettre sous ton oreiller ;
Et chaque matin à ton réveil
De ses couleurs te caresser.

J'aim'rai être celle qui est là
Quand tu es triste et solitaire,
Pouvoir faire toutes ces choses là
Et te chanter une rivière.

Ce n'est jamais une chose facile
De faire ce qui touche nos cœurs ;
Donc pour l'instant, d'mon domicile
Accepte moi, ouvre ton cœur.

C.D.B.

To Love Is to Give

I want to give you a mountain,
A place where you can be
Unafraid in peace and quiet
And bask in serenity.

I want to give you a rainbow,
Under your pillow a color bouquet,
Each morning when you awaken
To soften and brighten your day.

I want to be by your side
When the sad shadows are gray,
And sing you a happy song
To chase those shadows away.

Sometimes it is not easy
To do what touches the heart,
But now, from this moment in time,
Take my friendship and all it imparts.
C.D.B.

Quand tu n'es pas là

Je m'éteins comme étant au vide,
Ne pouvant boire le souffle de nos rêves,
Sans ton amour pour me donner la vie
Mon âme se fane tout en pleurant tes lèvres.

Quand tu n'es pas là, le soleil n'est plus,
Les oiseaux du ciel oublient leurs chansons.
Une nuit sans lune est intervenue
Cachant les étoiles au fond des buissons.

Un vieux chat miaule au bout des gouttières
Il accompagne mon ombre bien triste.
Je voudrais tant voir ce qu'était hier,
Quand tu étais, d'amour, un artiste.

A tout petits pas, dans des nuits trop blanches,
Mes larmes te cherchent, ne peuvent s'arrêter.
Milles pensées de toi tombent en avalanche
Dans un cœur si lourd et désorienté.

C.D.B.

When You're Away...

I fade into the space around me,
The breath of our dreams I miss,
Without your love to give it life
My withered soul cries for your kiss.

When you're away the sun will not shine,
The birds of heaven forget to sing,
The moon turns its back on the night,
Clouds cover the light that stars bring.

A cat's endless meows in the mist
Keep company with the shadow of me,
I'm caught in a web of the past,
In a time when your love set me free.

My tears are trying to find you,
Searching the white of the night,
A thousand thoughts of you, my dear,
Cry of my heart's lonely plight.

C.D.B.

Je veux être

Ton soleil couleur Topaze
Qui te sourit à ton réveil;
Et aussi, de ton café, la tasse
Qui doucement effleure tes lèvres.

Je veux être la douceur de laine
Du pull-over couvrant ton cœur,
Ton sang, vivre dans tes veines,
De tête aux pieds, nourrir ton corps.

Je veux être chaque mot d'amour
De ta bouche, pour l'embrasser.
Pourquoi pas, de tes yeux, le velours
Dans ton âme si douce me noyer.

Toute chose qui te touche, je veux être.
Dans le creux de tes bras me blottir,
Ne jamais entendre de peut-être,
Et sentir de nos cœurs les soupirs.

C.D.B.

I Want to Be...

...smiling at you when you waken
In the Topaz rays of the dawn,
The cup holding your coffee
That passes the depth of your yawn.

I want to be the softness of wool,
The warmth of your heart to keep,
The blood flowing through your veins
That reaches within you so deep.

I want to be the words of love
That come with each gentle kiss,
The color that brightens your eyes
And the place where your soul exists.

I want to be all around you,
Your warm presence is my sun,
I want only to hear of "forevers,"
And to feel our hearts sigh as one.

C.D.B.

Ce Soir

Ce soir, tu penseras à moi,
Revivant le silence nocturne d'un été,
Une Rose, une épine, nous avions rencontré.

Ce soir, me prenant dans tes bras,
Tes pensées brûlantes imaginant le feu
D'un amour platonique vivant entre nous deux.

Ce soir, je penserai à toi,
Je sentirai la fièvre surgissant d'un appel
De t'avoir près de moi, un désir surréel.

Ce soir, je penserai à toi,
Le souffle de ton cœur endormi dans mes rêves,
Deux larmes d'enfant ruisselantes sur mes lèvres.

Au matin, nous nous dirons bonsoir,
Dans un soleil perdu, au froid d'un nouveau jour,
Nous prierons pour que vienne une nuit de toujours.

C.D.B.

Tonight

Tonight you will think of me...
And you'll relive that sweet summer morn
When we met, you and I, rose and thorn.

Tonight I'll lie in your arms...
Your passion will burn bright in your mind
While our hearts crave to be intertwined.

Tonight, I will think of you...
The rising fever filling in my soul
And wishing for your touch to be whole.

Tonight, I will think of you...
To longing lips lonely tears will stream
While your heart's breath sleeps soft in my dream.

And we'll say goodnight at dawn...
In the first rays of morning's cold light
I'll pray to live the dream of last night.

C.D.B.

Si....

Si je m'éveille à ton côté
Voudras-tu me toucher?
De tes yeux dans mes yeux
Voudras-tu faire un vœu?

Dans une vague d'émotions
Un profond tourbillon,
Pourras-tu désarmer
Ce cœur qui veut t'aimer?

Si la foudre tombait
Sur notre beau Palais,
Serais-tu là, toujours
Protéger notre Amour?

Si à toutes ces questions
Avec Oui, tu réponds
Donc, je serais à Toi
Quand nous aurons le droit.

C.D.B.

If....

If I awake at your side,
Would you want to touch me now?
Would your eyes look into mine?
Would you want to make a vow?

When feelings overwhelm you
With swirling, deep emotions,
Could you possibly disarm
My heart filled with devotion?

If lightning were to strike us,
Bring to our palace a threat,
Could my heart depend on you
Our boundless love to protect?

If to each of these questions,
You can answer "yes" tonight,
I promise to be with you
As soon as we have the right.

C.D.B.

Quelque chose

Tu es Quelque chose, tu sais.
Chanson et refrain de mille nuits,
Musique d'un oiseau qui chantait,
La danse de mon cœur qui frémit.

Ce petit Quelque chose, tu sais.
Qui me donne dans la tête le tournis,
Et dans tes bras, me fait chavirer
Si souvent, quand tes yeux me sourient.

Cette belle grande chose, tu sais.
Tes mots doux au milieu d'un amour,
Tes baisers sous un ciel étoilé,
Tes caresses me donnant des toujours.

Tu es Quelque chose, tu sais.
A l'oiseau du matin je l'ai dit;
Autre chose n'aurait jamais suffit.
Tu es quelque chose, tu sais….

C.D.B.

Something

You are Something, you know,
Song of a thousand nights,
The music for birds to sing,
The dance of my heart's delight.

This small Something, you know,
Makes me all fuzzy and warm
Every time you smile at me
And I do a spin in your arms.

This great Something, you know,
Brings your kisses under the stars,
The love in your tender words,
Caresses that are just ours.

You are Something, you know,
I told the morning bird so,
Something else could not have been,
You are Something, you know....

C.D.B.

Toi

Je t'ai connu il y a longtemps,
Nos pensées croisant constamment.
Not mots de suite se sont aimés,
Puis, tant à dire, tant à chanter.

Au milieu de tout nos malheurs
Nous poursuivions le vrai bonheur.
De l'autre côté de la terre
Nous nous étions bien découverts.

Mais le temps nous trompe parfois,
Nous devons vivre sans toi et moi.
Te voilà à l'autre bout de ma vie,
Je prie souvent " Etre avec lui "

Le bonheur est comme un diamant
Qui sur mon cœur reste, brillant,
Il m'envoie tes rayons d'soleil
Que je lis dans les draps du ciel.

C.D.B.

You

I have known you forever,
Our loving thoughts cross constantly,
Our hearts sing out to each other,
Without words we speak endlessly.

In the mist of our aloneness
On continents so far apart,
We're longing to touch each other,
Soul mates seeking sweet joy of heart.

Time and circumstance betray us,
We must live without you and me,
At the far end of life you are,
And I wonder why we can't be.

Happiness is a diamond's gleam,
Brilliant facets upon my heart,
Sending shimmers of your sunshine,
Warming my soul though we're apart.

C.D.B.

L'aller-retour

Une dernière caresse, un dernier regard,
Tu étais si beau le jour du départ;
Dans tes yeux si tristes, je voulais plonger
Partir avec toi pour toujours rêver.

L'oiseau est venu t'arracher de moi,
Il t'a emmené au pays des Rois.
Au-dessus des eaux roulant de fureur,
Tu as disparu saisissant mon cœur.

Et depuis ce jour j'ai voulu trouver
Un visage aimant pour me retrouver
Dans tes bras, blottie sous une caresse,
Pour finir mes jours, doucement, sans stress.

Le jour du retour nous voit face à face,
Comment ce fait-il que l'av'nir se casse.
Avoir attendu si longtemps pour toi,
Ton regard figé m'a donné le froid.

Que s'est-il passé pendant ces années ?
Ils t'on fait du mal, t'on presque tué.
Tu ne peux pas voir mes larmes qui coulent,
Mon Amour pour toi est mis tout en boule.

Mais ta voix charmante est toujours la même,
Et tes mains si douces ont touché les miennes.
Du fond de mon âme à soudain surgit
Un Amour sans fin qui te donne la vie.

Dans notre chaumière nous vivrons heureux
Quelques rosiers jaunes, un hamac pour deux.
Je te cajolerai pour l'éternité…..
Et mes yeux jamais devront te quitter.

C.D.B.

Round Trip

A last caress, then a last look,
So handsome you are on this day,
Oh, how I long to stay with you...
Instead you are going away.

A silver bird steals you from me,
Taking flight to a distant land
Over angry, rolling waters,
You leave with my heart in your hand.

From the day we part, I'm waiting,
And searching each crowd for your face,
In your arms I yearn to cuddle,
Without worry to end my days.

At long last we find each other,
The future promises no bliss,
So long I've waited, but I get
Your blank look instead of a kiss.

Tell me, my love, what has happened,
You are hurt, you nearly have died,
You no longer can see my tears,
My sad heart's tied in knots inside.

Your sweet voice still sounds as it did,
And I know in this soul of mine
That my love can give you new life
As our fingers now intertwine.

In our cottage we'll be happy,
With roses and hammock for two,
For both of us my eyes will see,
And forever I will spoil you.

C.D.B.

Quand tu m'écris

Tes mots doux ont pris la forme
Des nuages d'un ciel d'été,
Ils sont caresses de tes mains folles
Que tu me donnes sans me toucher.

Ton long regard traverse la brume
Que ces nuages ont amassé,
Je l'entends rire, suivant ta plume
Dans mes yeux bleus vient s'y plonger.

Et tu écris, toujours, encore
Me nourrissant de ton amour,
Ton nom s'écrit en encre d'or
Car un Trésor, tu es, toujours.

C.D.B.

When You Write

Your sweet words bring me the softness
Of the clouds from a summer sky,
From your pen they are a caress,
Without a touch my heart soars high.

Transcending the fog of the clouds,
The dear thought you have written flies
Your pen brings a wave of laughter
And a bright twinkle deep in my eyes.

You write me again as always,
Loving words sent to nourish me,
Signing your name in golden ink,
For my treasure you'll always be.

C.D.B.

Parle Moi

Parle moi, dans le vent de l'automne,
Dans la voix vibrante du tremble d'or,
Le bruissement des feuilles me donne
Un gentil frisson qui me dit, encore.

Parle moi, dans les vagues de la mer,
Une voix si douce aux lèvres salées.
Dans son lit d'écume, une nuit m'y perdre
Et puis te retrouver au sable mouillé.

Parle moi, dans une pluie fine d'été
Une voix lente, mouillée de plaisir,
Rafraîchie ce soir mes sens épuisés,
Et de ton amour, me laisser mourir.

Parle moi, simplement, en disant:
"Je t'aime."

C.D.B.

Talk to Me

Talk to me in the breeze of autumn,
In the voice of a golden fall tree
Whose leaves whisper tender affections,
A rustle that says, "Come to me."

In the waves of the sea, talk to me,
Let their smooth, salty kiss my lips reach,
Bring me a night in its foamy bed,
Let me find you on a warm, wet beach.

Talk to me in the soft summer rain,
A slow voice soaking me with delight,
Refresh my exhausted senses,
Let me die in your arms tonight.

Talk to me simply by saying,
"I love You. "

C.D.B.

Otage

Sans même me le demander
Mon cœur tu as kidnappé.
Il cherchait un abri sûr,
Suivant ses jours de vie si dure.

Dans ce cachot qu'est ton amour
Il veut rester…pas de détour ;
Donc il me faut payer le prix,
Enorme rançon que tu as mise.

Pour finalement me libérer
Je me suis trouvée fermée
Dans une chambre pleine de soleil
Que tu me donnes à mon réveil.

Quelle douce vie cette prison,
Tu la remplies de longs frissons.
Et quand j'ai faim de tes baisers,
Tu me les donnes sans hésiter.

Et maintenant dans ce bonheur
Où se sont trouvés nos cœurs,
Tu peux garder la porte fermée
Dès aujourd'hui, jeter la clef.

C.D.B.

Hostage

You did not ask my permission
When my trusting heart you stole,
It was only seeking refuge
After heartbreak took its toll.

In this prison that you call love
My heart has chosen to bask,
So I'm required to pay the price,
The huge ransom you have asked.

In order to gain my freedom,
To your love I am locked in,
A room filled with the warm sun
You give me on wakening.

What a sweet place, this prison cell,
This life sentence I have incurred,
When I hunger for your kisses,
You feed me and make me purr.

And now in this great happiness
Where our hearts have come together,
The door's locked tight with your caress,
And the key you hid forever.

C.D.B.

Ouïe, j'écoute

Bien sûr, téléphone moi,
Laisse moi entendre ta voix.
Dis-moi que tout va bien
Dans ton pays si lointain.

Donne-moi de tes nouvelles,
Dis-moi que la mer est belle
A l'Est de mes montagnes.
Je suis toute oreille, toute âme.

Te sens-tu désorienté?
Toi qui serais ma moitié,
Ton cœur est-il prêt à venir
Dans mon nid vide, me secourir?

Fais vibrer aujourd'hui cet appareil
Ce téléphone qui fait la veille;
Oh ! Oh !...Je dois quitter ma plume
J'entends sonner...Toi, je présume.
Merci, Mr. Bell.

C.D.B.

I Am Listening...

I wish you would call me,
Your voice I need to hear...
Is it good where you are?
Will you soon be near?

Give me some wonderful news
From your distant mountain land,
Tell me of the ocean's shore,
I'm all ears, I'll understand.

Do you feel bewilderment?
Or, like I do, hopelessness?
Is your heart on its way here
To free me from loneliness?

Today, please make my phone ring,
Its loud silence fills the room,
Oh! Oh! I have to leave my pen,
I hear a ring...You, I presume.
Thank you, Mr. Bell.

C.D.B.

Quel âge avons-nous ?

L'âge de vivre au plein,
De sentir et saisir nos matins,
A pleine bouche les croquer, c'est vrai
Avant qu'ils se ferment à jamais.

L'âge de créer notre paradis
Au son des jours qui sont écrits,
Pleins de sourires et de soleils
Quand, d'amour, nous battons des ailes.

L'âge du souvenir venu d'hier
Quand nous étions, oh oui, si fiers
De raconter tous nos exploits
A quiconque ne nous croyait pas.

L'âge de s'asseoir et de penser
Combien cette vie nous a donné;
En gardant cet amour précieux
Comme s'il était un dernier vœu.

C.D.B.

How Old Are We?

Old enough to live to the full,
To reach out and seize each day,
To savor the morsels of time
Before they all fade away.

Old enough to write our paradise
In the pages recording our days,
To fill them with smiles and sunshine,
To share love in so many ways.

Old enough for fond memories
For pride in what we have done,
To tell of life's battles we've fought
And of the victories we've won.

Old enough to contemplate
This precious gift life offers,
Our dear love that we keep safe
Within our own hearts' coffers.

C.D.B.

Jamais... Stop... Toujours... Encore

Si Jamais sans toi, me trouvant seule,
Sans espoir, nulle, noyée de pleurs;
Sous la mousse sèche je glisserai
Un soleil gris et froid me couvrirait.

Stop ici, n'y penses même pas,
Une promesse ne suffit pas
Car notre amour est véritable
Nous danserons jusqu'au Népal.

Toujours, pour être à ton côté,
A tes désirs je suis vouée;
Sous les rayons de lune d'argent
Tu m'aimeras jusqu'au levant.

Encore, encore redis-les moi
Ces mots qui tremblent dans ta voix;
Dans les pâquerettes je suis tombée,
De ton amour je suis comblée.

Jamais Stop ce besoin d'être aimée,
Toujours Encore dans les saisons de blé,
Nous vivrons des soupirs et des larmes
De deux cœurs que la passion désarme.

C.D.B.

Never…Stop…Always…Again

"Never" do I want to lose you,
To hopelessly drown in my tears,
Away from the world I would hide
And under gray skies spend my years.

"Stop" here! Don't even think of it!
Mere promises will never do!
Our true love deserves so much more,
A heart's waltz for our whole lives through.

"Always" I will be at your side
To please you with my sweet surrender,
And in the soft silver moonlight
You'll love me until the dawn's splendor.

"Again" and again, say to me,
With your heart trembling in your words,
While in the daisies I am falling,
With your love I fly with the birds.

"Never Stop" this need for our love,
"Always Again" in ev'ry season
Our hearts meld in sighs and in tears
To which our sweet passion gives reason.

C.D.B.

Une vie Irrésistible

Quelques fois rose, quelques fois bleue,
Odeur lilas, odeur des cieux.
Très souvent une envie d'rire
Toujours donnant un beau sourire.

On la croque à p'tites bouchées,
Quand on est jeune on est pressés;
Mais quand l'âge d'or est à la porte
On la retient d'une main bien forte.

Quand un amour dans le cœur naît
On veut la prendre et la donner,
Pour partager chaque jour fleuri,
La Vie devient Irrésistible.

Irrésistible tu l'es aussi.
De lilas roses tu peins ma vie.
Et puis je vois tout est possible,
Dans notre amour irrésistible.

C.D.B.

Irresistible Life

Sometimes in pink, sometimes in blue,
Lilac scented from heaven, too,
Life often wants to laugh out loud
And often smiles down from a cloud.

Little by little we taste of it,
As rushing youths, we get just a bit,
But when golden age is at the door,
We try to hold it and long for more.

When in our heart a love is born,
Life becomes a spanking spring morn,
Each fresh new day we want to share...
Irresistibility there.

Irresistible are your ways,
With pink lilacs you paint my days,
Then I can see just what can be...
Your irresistible love for me.

C.D.B.

Les Vagabondes

Elles semblent être sans foyer,
Toujours cherchant un abri,
Et elles essayent de dépouiller
Ce qui appartient à autrui.

Elles peuvent écrire des mots suaves
Et faire gémir sans pitié,
Avec leurs doigts elles sont sauvages,
Et toujours veulent se cacher.

Douces elles sont, petites coquines,
Sous la dentelle elles vagabondent
Les combattre n'est pas facile
Je sens la chaleur qui monte….
De tes Mains.

C.D.B.

The Vagabonds

They appear to be homeless,
Always looking for cover,
And then they try to pilfer
That which belongs to others.

Smooth words they can write
To fill eyes with tears,
With fingers so wild
Where they should not appear.

Such sweet little rascals,
Under soft lace disguising,
Saying "no" isn't easy,
And I feel the heat rising...
From your hands.

C.D.B.

Clameur de silence

As-tu parlé au vent du soir?
Il te dira que je suis seule;
Il te donnera une bonne histoire
En gémissant dans les Tilleuls.

Il demandera que tu écoutes
La rivière nue dans ses torrents;
Qui t'emmèn'ra sans aucun doute
A ma chaumière et dans mes champs.

Au beau milieu de cette verdure
Tu pourras prendre ton élan,
Et me chanter ces mots si purs
Qui guériront ce cœur aimant.

Le rossignol d'une nuit d'été,
Sous le regard d'une lune sournoise,
Chante le refrain d'un cœur aimé,
La paix d'Amour venant de toi.

C.D.B.

Clamor of Silence

Did you speak to the wind of the night?
Did it tell you I was alone?
It will relate a story
While through the trees it groans.

It will ask you to stop and listen
To the river's torrents and sounds
As it brings you here to my cottage,
'Cross my fields and over my ground.

In the middle of this beauty
You'll be able to gather speed,
As you bring your sweet words to me
To heal this heart in love indeed.

A nightingale on a summer's eve
Under the sly eye of the moon,
Sings me the song from your heart,
Your love in its tranquil tune.

C.D.B.

Tout comme çà

Ne plus aimer, j'ai décidé,
C'est devenu trop difficile.
Mon cœur n'arrête de saigner
En me disant que c'est facile.

Je ne voulais plus lui écrire
Même ignorer toutes ses lettres.
Voulant m'efforcer à revivre
Et me donner une raison d'être.

Au revoir nuits noires et blanches
Finalement je peux dormir.
Et soudain, un son étrange,
Un appel me fait sourire.

L'Amour est une vraie maladie
Et qui en connaît le remède?
De l'aimer plus encore, je dis
Est le moyen de m'en remettre.

C.D.B.

Just Like That

I decided to love no more,
It became too much to bear,
I bled with the pain of heartbreak
Because I ventured to care.

I wanted to stop writing
Or even your letters read,
I wanted to live again
And to my own life give heed.

Good-bye to nights dark and sleepless,
At long last I can get some rest,
A sound and my eyes open wide
A call and again I'm restless.

Is love a disease of the heart?
Do you know the best remedy?
To get well I must love even more,
So please bring your love back to me.

C.D.B.

Courrier du Cœur

Je t'écris d'un pays de pluie
Où j'ai déposé ma tristesse.
Ma vie semblait être finie,
Et mon cœur pleurait sans cesse.

Je t'écris d'un pays de soleil
Où j'ai trouvé un rayon d'amour.
Ma vie est devenue merveille,
Pleine de bonheur jusqu'à ce jour.

Je t'écris d'un pays d'arc-en-ciel
Où j'ai pu te donner mon cœur.
De l'aube rose, au coucher du soleil
Tu me baignes dans ta douceur.

C.D.B.

100

Love Mail

I'm writing from a land of rainfall
Where I have let all my sadness go,
My life seemed to end in this place
With the tears of my broken heart's woe.

I'm writing from a land of sunshine,
A ray of love I have found,
My life has become the summer
To share with you in sweet sound.

I'm writing from a land of rainbows,
Where now my happy heart sings,
At sunrise or sunset I am yours,
My joy your sweet love will bring.

C.D.B.

Reprise

Sur les miettes de mes rêves je vivrais,
Ils sont pour moi de vrais délices.
Ils me donnent sans cesse tes lèvres
Dont j'ai si soif ; eau de mélisse.

Sans le plaisir de te toucher
Une fièvre me tenant compagnie
Continuera à m'envelopper,
Dans mon cœur, l'amour fait son nid.

Peut-être un jour tu comprendras
Combien tu es, de loin, "moi-même "
Sans ma moitié je ne vis pas
Je suis seulement celle qui t'aime.

Un nouveau jour viendra, c'est sûr
En attendant tes mots si doux,
Et je verrai tes yeux si purs
Regard d'amour, sans aucun doute.

C.D.B.

I Will Survive

I will live on the crumbs of my dreams,
For to me they are a delight.
They bring me the warmth of your kiss,
Quench my thirst for your love tonight.

I've not known the joy of your touch,
But my love burns brightly for you,
Wrapping me in a dream of your presence
Where my heart will forever be true.

Someday you may come to know
How much you are part of me,
Without you I'm just a shadow
Of love that is waiting to be.

But a new day will come, I am sure,
When sweet words of devotion you'll say,
And you'll give me a look pure and soft
As your love you are sending my way.
C.D.B.

Le Blues du Sax

Ecoute cette musique lente et profonde,
Elle parle de la tristesse qui m'inonde.
Les horizons du monde étaient à nous,
Nous aurions pu nous rendre fous.

Tes yeux d'amour tu as changé,
Tu n'étais jamais rassasié,
De tes demandes trop exigeantes
J'étais lassée, souvent mourante.

Des sables mouvants sur lesquels tu marchais,
J'ai du m'éloigner et choisir la paix.
Désolée mon grand, mais si je pardonne
Tu feras de moi un vrai....Sex-aphone.

C.D.B.

Sad Song

Hear this, my sad, lonely song
That speaks of the pain within me,
We had the world in our hands,
A thousand dreams we knew could be.

Your loving ways toward me have changed,
You who once begged for my heart
Now *demand* what you think you are due,
Not caring if *I* fall apart.

The lover who nurtured my spirit,
Whose gentleness I learned to trust,
Brings my tears from his selfish acts,
For his sweet love has turned to lust.

C.D.B.

Douceur du Moment

D'un regard languissant
Un amour peut germer.
L'arroser tendrement
De musique enchantée.

Un dialogue de silence
Peut faire fleurir les cœurs,
Réveiller tous les senses
Au parfum de mille fleurs.

De sentir la chaleur
D'une main dans la mienne,
A bien plus de valeur
Que le ciel du septième.

Et simplement savoir
Qu'un cœur précieux vous aime,
Non seulement pour avoir
Mais pour la joie qu'il sème.

C.D.B.

Sweet Moment

From a look that cherishes
A lasting love can grow
If it's nurtured tenderly
With song to soothe the soul.

A dialogue of silence
Can bind two hearts like ours,
Awakening the senses
With the scent of many flowers.

Just to feel the warmth
Of your dear hand in mine
Is more to be desired
Than a ticket to cloud nine.

Knowing you have given me
Your precious love so true,
Brings the pleasure of receiving
And of giving back to you.

C.D.B.

Myosotis

Si jamais tu partais,
D'ici jusqu'à toujours,
Peut-être j'en mourrais
Je n' veux pas voir ce jour.

Rappelles-toi de ces années
Qui devaient être les nôtres,
Garde les dans tes pensées
Et aussi d'un cœur à l'autre.

Rappelles-toi nos rêves tendres
Qui nous faisaient trembler,
Et de loin pour les entendre
Nous devions communiquer.

Peux-tu, chéri, te rapprocher,
Ma vie à l'abri dans ta main,
Tout doucement la cajoler
Et ne jamais voir un demain.

Ne m'oublie pas, " Myosotis "
C.D.B.

Forget-Me-Not

If ever you would leave me,
I could not bear the pain
I would rather die
Than be alone again.

Remember all the years
That ours are meant to be,
Safeguard them in your dreams
And keep your love for me.

Recall the tender words
That once made us shiver,
Commit them to memory
Like arrows in a quiver.

Shelter me in your arms,
Take my life in your hand,
Forever sing our love song,
Let our future fill the land.

Always remember...forget me not!

C.D.B.

Si j'étais Toi...

Je comprendrai le mot aimer,
Je toucherai d'un doigt léger
L'amour profond qu'elle veut donner.

Si j'étais Toi ...
Des mots de cœur, douceur de miel
Seraient toujours versés sur elle,
Ne faire pleurer, jamais, ma belle.

Si j'étais Toi...
De ses yeux bleus je pourrai voir
Jour après jour, un désespoir
D'amour fané, dans un vide noir.

Si j'étais Toi...
Je me pos'rai un tas d'questions,
Me rappelant où nous étions,
Et puis me dire "Fais attention."

Si j'étais Toi...
J'apprécierai une âme pudique,
D'esprit chanteur et romantique,
Vêtue de rêves, simples et uniques.

Mais je suis Moi.

C.D.B.

If I Were You...

The word Love I would understand,
With gentleness I would reach out
For the heart that's in her hand.

If I were you...
Winsome words from my lips would fall,
Overflowing with love and joy
And would never bring tears at all.

If I were you...
I would see the pain in her eyes so blue,
The despair that's growing each day
From the dearth of love overdue.

If I were you...
I would ask myself many questions,
Remembering what we have shared,
I would say to me, "Pay attention."

If I were you...
I would treasure the love she brings,
Her spirit soft with hopes and dreams,
I would hear the song she sings.

But I am Me.

C.D.B.

Prend ma main

Conduit-moi au silence de tes rêves
Sans un mot, sans un bruit.
Seul le murmure de tes lèvres
Adoucit mon cœur, le rend soumis.

Des couloirs de ma solitude
Tu m'as retirée tremblante,
Ayant en moi l'incertitude,
Ne sachant de quoi m'attendre.

Marchant main dans la main
Dans l'ombre de tes pensées,
Avant l'arrivée du matin
Est-il l'heure de nous aimer ?

Un rêve ne compte pas sur l'orage
Que les pluies du passé mijotaient,
N'étant préparés pour cet outrage,
Nous sommes noyés dans le marais.

C.D.B.

Take My Hand

In the silence of your dreams
With neither word nor sound
But the whisper of your lips,
You touch the heart you've found.

From the corridors of solitude
I emerge with trepidation,
Following you uncertainly,
Growing faint with expectation.

Walking hand in hand with you
In the shadow of your dreams,
Is it time for us to love?
Is that part of your scheme?

A dream ignores the storms
And the rain that's all around,
We have no umbrella...
Could it be that we have drowned?

C.D.B.

Maladie d'amour

Je crois souffrir du mal d'amour,
Ou peut-être d'un mal de tête.
Non, c'est sûr, j'ai le cœur lourd
Comment arrêter cette tempête?

Voyons, maint'nant, que pourrais-je faire?
Pour supprimer cette maladie,
Elle me fait mal, comment me taire ?
Je veux pleurer et rire aussi.

Les jours repassent, les nuits sont longues,
Je vois les soleils et les pluies.
Est-il quelqu'un loin de mes songes?
Peut-il de suite me réjouir?

Oh ! Oui, bien sûr, écoute cette voix,
Fleur de printemps et de bonheur,
Elle est très douce, elle vient de Toi,
Elle seule peut sécher ma douleur.

Et soudainement des pleurs de joie
Très vite, s'écoulant de mes yeux,
Un drôle d'effet tu as sur moi,
Dis-moi, quand deviendras-tu sérieux?

C.D.B.

Lovesick

I think that I am love-sick,
Or maybe it's a headache,
I'm sure my heart is ailing,
This time there's no mistake.

Let me see what can I do
To cure what makes me ill,
It hurts...I can't be fooled,
Do I need to take a pill?

Nights are long, days are grim,
I see many suns and rains,
Is there someone in my dreams
Who can bring about a change?

Just in time I hear a tune,
Soft words, a happy song,
It is sweet, it comes from you,
And I want to sing along.

A flow of joy comes suddenly,
No more tears...I am delirious,
What a strange effect you have on me —
Do you think it will be serious?

C.D.B.

La femme inachevée

Elle marche le cœur tranquille
Dans les jours du passé,
Quand elle traverse la ville
Les murs semblent crier.
Ils connaissent cette image
Qui va d'un pas léger.
Elle peut tromper un sage
Mais elle manque de gaîté.

Cette vision de douceur,
Un secret dans le sang;
Tant d'amour dans le cœur
Mais perdu dans le vent.
Les yeux vides elle sourit
Aux passants qui la guettent;
Si seulement ce ciel gris
La faisait disparaître.

Dans un coin quelque part
Existe un être aimé,
Touchera sans retard
Cette femme inachevée.

C.D.B.

Unfinished Woman

She comes with unfulfilled heart,
A shadow from days gone by,
When she appears downtown
The walls begin to cry;
They know well her image
Walking with stride so light,
She fools others, however wise,
But she knows there's no joy in sight.

This vision of sweet womanhood
Hides a secret deep in her soul,
The love she's kept in her heart
Finds no home on her stroll;
With a blank look she smiles
To passersby on her way;
Lost in the wind and gray skies,
Her heart's lonely another day.

Somewhere out there in the city
He waits for her walk on his street,
His lifetime of sweet love will make
This unfinished woman complete.

C.D.B.

Mes Amis Intimes

Mes Poèmes sont mes compagnons,
Ils gardent gentiment mes Rêves,
Ils sont une célébration
De mes moments les plus chers.

Sur papier, collection de mots.
Dans mes pensées, joies à revivre.
De mon cœur, ils enlèvent les maux;
Intimes ils sont, je peux vous l'dire !

Mes compagnons prennent soin de moi,
Me donnent l'amour dont j'ai besoin,
D'une manière différente je crois
Mais faute du vrai, c'est pas vilain.

C.D.B.

My Intimate Friends

My poems are my companions,
They keep safe my dreams,
They are a celebration
Of my dearest joys and schemes.

The words upon my pages
Relive my thoughts and deeds.
In my heart they salve the wounds,
Intimate they are indeed!

My companions care for me,
They make my life complete,
In their way they bring me love,
Good or not, they are so sweet.

C.D.B.

Créativité

Un mot très puissant,
La muse du poète,
Il la boit et la sent
Et la porte dans sa tête.

Elle est toujours vibrante
Lui fait briller les yeux,
Avec une voix charmante
Elle le rend Amoureux.

Dans ses ballades aux bois
Et au milieu des prés,
Il devient vite sa proie
Pour écrire ses versets.

Mais quelle beauté elle donne
Au poète plein d'amour,
Quand ses mots il fredonne
Et refait plusieurs tours.

Créativité fait de nous
Des artistes c'est certain,
Quand nous laissons l'amour
Nous prendre aux lendemains.

C.D.B.

Creativity

This very powerful muse
Is the poet's friend,
He drinks it and he feels it,
It's the means to reach his end.

She is always vibrant,
She can wrap him in her arms,
Make him fall in love,
Beguile him with her charms.

By the lake or in the woods,
He takes a gentle stroll,
Then she comes to him in verse
And quickly takes her toll.

To a poet who's in love,
Her happy words he's humming,
What beauty she then gives
When the page his pen is strumming.

Creativity is the artist
That brings color, texture, too,
It opens up tomorrows
When love the heart renews.

C.D.B.

Other Fine Publications from Edit et Cetera Ltd.

KATHERINE'S SONG by Linda Lane. (Nov. 2003) Katherine Kohler has it all...a loving husband, a wonderful family, a great job...everything she ever wanted. But it ends when her dear Edmund dies tragically, leaving her the family business. Now she must honor a promise that takes her in a direction she never wanted to go.

She reels with pain when her younger daughter blames her for Ed's death. Then she learns that, on the last day he lived, her husband made an offer to her despised brother-in-law. And *she's* expected to fulfill it.

Oren Kohler looks enough like his deceased brother to be his twin, but there the similarity ends. A manipulative opportunist with a diabolical mind, a chip on his shoulder, and a vendetta against women, he has come to settle an old score with his sister-in-law.

The secret Oren has kept from all of them adds another ingredient to the mix that threatens to destroy everything that was dear to his brother. Will Katherine overcome her grief in time to mend her relationship with her daughter, save the family business, and reach our for a new life of her own?

A must-read for lovers of compelling stories and family-oriented fiction.

GRAND RIVER STUDENT ANTHOLOGY 2004 (May 2004) Working in conjunction with Mesa State College professor, poet, and owner of Farolito Press, Dr. L. Luis Lopez, and Marco Weber of Readmoor Books, Edit et Cetera Ltd. published the works of some 200 students in the Grand Valley, a region that includes Grand Junction, Colorado, and surrounding areas.

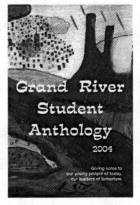

Inundated with several hundred entries from hopeful students, grades K-12, we were assisted with the difficult process of choosing those papers that would become part of this pilot project by a panel of Mesa State honors students. Even our cover was designed by a seventh-grader. After publication, we held a full day of readings, during which time more than half of those published read their works in front of family and friends who came to applaud their efforts.

The students who submitted entries for this anthology touched our hearts with their insight, their honesty, their hopes, their pain, their dreams, and their writing ability. We salute them! At Edit et Cetera Ltd. we encourage reading at all ages and advocate the advancement of literacy worldwide.

RAGAMUFFINS OF THE FIFTH WARD by **Charles S. Novinskie.**
(Scheduled for publication: Fall 2004) The 1960s—
a wondrous era of comic books, baseball, marbles,
trading cards, skateboards, candy, and buzz hair-
cuts—were permeated with a kind of naïveté. Kids
could be kids during this carefree, laid-back time.
Growing up seemed light years away.

Comic books cost 12¢ and were sheer magic to
be read and reread, then folded up and placed in back
pockets to be traded and read again and again. Kids
bought baseball cards as much for the stick of hard,
pink gum as for the cards themselves. Candy, sold
loose in bulk quantities, didn't wear today's win-
something-free gimmicky wrappers.

Being kids meant fun unhindered by adult intrusions. They could amuse
themselves all day long without fear of getting in trouble—or worse, some-
thing terrible happening to them.

The lazy days of summer were just that, but nobody ever had more fun
or expended more energy doing absolutely nothing. Fond memories of kids
being kids in a northeastern coal mining community during the sixties is
recaptured in this series of vignettes depicting life in those simpler times.

LOOKING FOR OUR PUBLICATIONS?

- Visit our website at www.familybookhouse.com
- Ask your favorite bookstore to order our books. They are distri-
  buted by Ingram's and by Baker and Taylor and are available
  to bookstores and libraries from these sources.
- Our publications are also available on amazon.com. You can
  search by title or by author.